The *Power* of POSITIVE THINKING

Your Ultimate Guide to Finding Success and Happiness in Life

author or copyright owner. Legal action will be pursued if this is breached.

Disclaimer Notice:

Please note the information contained within this document is for educational and entertainment purposes only. Every attempt has been made to provide accurate, up to date and reliable complete information. No warranties of any kind are expressed or implied. Readers acknowledge that the author is not engaging in the rendering of legal, financial, medical or professional advice.

By reading this document, the reader agrees that under no circumstances are we responsible for any losses, direct or indirect, which are incurred as a result of the use of information contained within this document, including, but not limited to, — errors, omissions, or inaccuracies.

TABLE OF CONTENTS

Introduction 6

Chapter 1 10

How Positive Thinking Works 10

How Do Happy People Find Good In The World? 11

Decide To Be Happy 13

Positive Attitude In Action 14

Our Minds Create Our World 17

Chapter 2 20

Benefits Of Having A Positive Thinking 20

Positive Thinkers Cope Better With Stress 20

Optimism Can Improve Your Immunity 21

Positive Thinking Is Good For Your Health 22

It Can Make You More Resilient 23

You Have Better Relationships With People 24

More Focused And Concentrated 25

More Confidence 25

They Have A Happier Life 26

Chapter 3 29

How to Recognize "BLUE" Thoughts 29

Blaming Myself 30

Looking For The Bad News 31

Unhappy Guessing 32

Exaggeratedly Negative 33

Chapter 4 36

What Negative Thoughts Do To Your Brain 36

The Link Between Thinking and Actions 39

Chapter 5 43

Tips to Train Your Mind for Positive Thoughts 43

Subconscious Retraining 43

Set Aside Specific Time for What You Love 44

Take Good Care Of Yourself 45

Give Positivity To Feel The Positivity 46

Focus On What Makes You Happy To Be Alive 47

Flip Negatives Into Positives 48

Chapter 6 50

The Role Of The Language We Use 50

Positive Language 51

Positive And Negative Language And The Brain 52

Characteristics Of Positive Thinking 54

Monitoring Your Self-Talk 54

Establishing A Psychological Space 55

Positive Responses 56

Become A Positive Contagion 56

The Importance of Positive Language 57

The Relationship Between Positive Thinking and a Positive Attitude .. 58

Chapter 7 62

Steps On How To Train Your Mind To Think Positive 62

Step 1: Observe Your Thoughts 62

Step 2: Scan For The Three Daily Positives 63

Step 3: Give Someone A Shout-Out 64

Step 4: Help Others 65

Step 5: Surround Yourself With Positive People 65

Step 6: Look After Your Body And Mind 66

Step 7: Let Go Of All The Negativity So That You Can Have Inner Healing 67

Step 8: Make Time To Do Something That You Love 68

Chapter 8 .... **70**

Thinking Systems For Success – Planning Positive Future ... 70

Addressing Failure 72

Developing A Winning Formula.. **73**

Establishing Your Systems..75

Understanding And Assessing Your Process............................76

Studying Others And Their Actions 76

Anticipating Challenges..77

Conclusion **79**

Introduction

Do you view yourself as someone who has a positive outlook on life? Do you hope that good things are coming your way soon? Well, one thing that is important to note is that positive thinking is a mental and emotional attitude. It pays a closer focus and interest on the bright side of life with the hope of having a positive outcome.

Having positive thinking does not mean that you should bury your head in the sand. It does not mean that you should ignore life's painful and unpleasant situations. It simply means having the ability to approach life more positively and productively even in the face of unpleasantness. Even when things are not going your way, you keep your head up and look for hidden lessons and opportunities in bad situations!

It is important for you to notice that you have the power to change your mindset. It all starts with self-talk. In other words, you must begin by stimulating endless streams of positive thoughts running through your head. The truth is, these thoughts can take two forms; the negative and the positive mainly because most of what you think are derived from logic and reason. However, other self-talks may arise from having misconceptions and assumptions that result from a lack of information.

If you mostly have negative thoughts running through your mind, most likely you are a pessimist. On the other hand, if most of the thoughts you have about life are mostly positive, there is a good chance that you are an optimist. In other words, you are someone that exercises positive thinking.

When you focus on the positive, you will mentally anticipate good health, success, and happiness. You believe that even when faced with the most challenging and difficult situations, you will eventually overcome them. In other words, having positive thinking is not a concept that everyone believes in. Some people will see it as nonsense and scoff at those that believe in the power of positive thinking. The good news is that there are so many people who are slowly seeing the important role that positive thinking has on their lives and believe that it is effective.

One thing that you must bear in mind is that if you want to use the power of positive thinking in your life, you must be more than just aware of the fact that it exists. You must be ready to adopt it in all your daily activities! There is so much research that reveals that positive thinking is not just about happiness and having an upbeat attitude. It is through positive thinking that you can create real value in your life by establishing long-lasting skills that last longer than a mere smile.

CHAPTER 1

HOW POSITIVE THINKING WORKS

Chapter 1

How Positive Thinking Works

When you think about the things that your heart desires and the ways you can get them, there is a stream of joy that comes from deep within you that makes you take great control of your life. It is like when you think of something or someone that makes you happy, your brain releases endorphins, that gives you that feeling of joy and happiness. It is these things that help us develop a positive attitude.

According to so many psychological studies, happy people have been shown to have a special quality that allows them to live a better-quality life compared to those who are not. What do you think is the reason for this? Well, the answer is simple. Optimism.

The good news about optimism is that you can learn it. In other words, you can train yourself to have positive thinking by simply adopting a mindset full of optimism. According to the law of cause and effect, if you emulate what successful and happy people do, you will start feeling the same and get the outcome they have, hence end up enjoying same experiences as they do.

How Do Happy People Find Good In The World?

One thing that you must realize is that optimistic people tend to handle things differently from average people and those who are pessimistic. The first thing is that they focus their minds on the things they want and then work hard to find ways to get those things. In other words, you need to ensure that your goals are clear and have the confidence that no matter how long it will take, you will work hard to accomplish them.

Secondly, optimistic people see the good in every situation, however difficult it may seem. It is important to bear in mind that things will go wrong at some point in your life and trust me, that is a good thing! In every difficult situation, there is a dark side and a bright side, and you are the one that will determine what direction you would like to follow. The most important thing is for you to see the positive.

Instead of always looking for an excuse not to like something, choose to see the good in everything. Even in that job that you may seem not to like so much, there is something good in it, and if you look carefully, you will find it. The thing is, while you look, you will become more positive and happier.

Positive thinking only works when you train your mind to be positive and to have an attitude that you can achieve whatever you want in life. The truth is, the mind has been created to have adequate bandwidth to pay attention to one thing at a time. Your job is to keep your mind focused on thoughts that lift you long enough to create neural pathways that help in establishing a new habit.

When you start facing a negative situation or event along the way, just remember that what matters most is how you respond to the situation. In other words, it is your response that will influence the outcome. It means that you must find a positive response even when things are not looking up. You can come up with positive affirmations or phrases you can repeat in your mind over and over so that you can overcome negative thoughts. It is this kind of words that will encourage you to have a positive attitude.

Decide To Be Happy

Being happy and living a positive life is a decision that you make. You can choose to see things as glass half empty or half full. Yes, things may not always fall in place. Bad situations will happen to you at some point in life, but that does not mean that you will never have it all. No one can say their life has always been a straight line. You will have some mountains, hills, and valleys along the journey of life. The trick is for you to enjoy every season and choose to count your blessings one by one instead of complaining about what did not go your way.

The people around you will, at some point, disappoint you, but that does not mean that they are bad people or that they hate you. When you look at everyone, choose to see the best intentions on their part. Trust me, most people are striving hard to do the best the way they could. Instead of focusing on that small thing they said that you did not like, why not look at the many good actions and words they have done to you before.

Finally, no matter what happens, decide to remain cheerful. In every situation, there is a hidden blessing underneath it. Your job is to find it!

Positive Attitude In Action

If there is anything life has taught each one of us is that when things are going well, it is easy to be happy. However, when we face unexpected setbacks our faith is put to the test. It is during difficulties that we demonstrate to ourselves and the world around us what our true attitude is. Ensure that what you portray is a positive one.

Choosing to have a positive attitude will help you in more ways than you can imagine. When you think positively, your mind, whether conscious or subconscious, will not be able to entertain any negative thoughts or doubts. Once you learn how to think positively, there are so many amazing changes that will happen in your life.

Your brain will begin to operate a state of the abundant flow of feel-good hormones. It will make you feel like a heavy burden has been lifted off your shoulders and suddenly you are light again. Additionally, you will notice a major boost in confidence, and you will take on tough assignments that are outside your zone of comfort.

When you reduce your self-limiting thoughts, you release the brakes you have applied in your life and suddenly experience new levels of growth you have never imagined possible. In other words, when you harness the power of positive thinking, you change your whole life.

Let us consider a real-life example of the power of positive thinking.

A child runs outside to play with friends. It is through their running that they develop athletic skills. Interacting with friends through play helps the child develop a team spirit and effective communication skills. Their ability to explore the world around them goes a long way in building their creative skills. It is the simple act of playing with others that helps build the child into a holistic individual equipped with skills that are valuable in their day to day life.

The truth is, it is these skills that last much longer than the emotion that stirred it up in the first place. Years down the line, it may be this athletic skill that will land them a scholarship as a college athlete, or their team spirit and communication skills that will help them do well in their role as a senior managing partner.

According to Fredrickson, this is referred to as the "broaden and build theory". This is because, when you have a positive emotion just like a child, your sense of possibilities will broaden, and you'll have a more opened mind. This, in turn, goes a long way in helping you build new skillsets that will prove to be valuable later in life.

Our Minds Create Our World

Look around you. What can you see?

The truth is everything that you see around you, whether a chair or a human being, has been created and first perceived by the mind of an individual. In other words, whatever your mind can conceive and believe, it can simply come into being. Well, some people may think that this is a poor positive thinking strategy that you have heard of over and over again. Up to this time, we had not been able to scientifically prove the power of positive thinking. However, today we can do that with the help of quantum physics.

What quantum physics has unraveled to us about the human mind, perception, and beliefs about reality is that you can use your mind to alter reality to perfectly fit your viewpoint.

For instance, so many scientists have demonstrated that the universe is made from particles while another group argued that it is made from waves. After many years of arguments, they all decided to take a step back so that they can have a different perspective. It is then that they discovered that the universe was created from waves or particles based on the scientists' expectations. If they expected that the world was formed from waves, that is exactly what they would see. And if they thought it was formed from waves, that is exactly what it appeared to be.

In the same manner, you continue to believe that reality is as it is because you think that certain things are beyond your control. However, the truth is, the reality is as it is because you expect it to be that way. Funny huh?

Well, this same concept explains the reason why so many successful people place so much importance on the power of their minds and thoughts. In other words, they create their realities by what they believe and then go ahead to put their efforts on cultivating their mindset. This is what eventually leads them to phenomenal success and joy. Then you wonder why the average person blames other people for their circumstances and failures. The secret is to look deep inside for the source of both failure and success.

The important question here is, "if your success in life is based on your mindset, what are you going to do about it?"

CHAPTER **2**

BENEFITS OF HAVING A
POSITIVE THINKING

Chapter 2

Benefits Of Having A Positive Thinking

Optimism is a virtue that is often portrayed as bringing happiness and fullness into life, and truth be told, these are not just words. There are so many benefits that positive thinking brings to our lives; health, relationships, confidence, among others. If you are not a positive thinker yet, here are some of the reasons why you should embrace a positive mindset.

Positive Thinkers Cope Better With Stress

It is normal to go through seasons of hardships in life. However, it is only a positive thinker that can effectively cope with the stressful situation compared to a pessimist. According to one research study, when an optimist encounters a challenging situation, they are highly likely to focus on the things they can do to solve the problem at hand.

Instead of dwelling on your disappointments and frustrations, it is important that you devise a plan of action or seek help from people who can advise or help.

Optimism Can Improve Your Immunity

Based on recent research studies, the mind has been shown to have a very powerful effect on the body. One of these effects is on the immunity of your body. One study demonstrated that when certain areas of our brain associated with negative emotions are activated, the immune response of the body to a flu vaccine is weakened.

Additionally, research studies have also shown that if you are optimistic about a certain thing in your life, for instance how well you do in school, the immune response is strengthened compared to those who have a negative perception of the whole situation.

The truth is, having a positive outlook on life, plays a critical role in helping us cope with stress and in boosting our immunity, hence our overall well-being. Other findings by the Mayo Clinic report that having a positive outlook lowers the risk of death from heart disease, reduces chances of having depression, and generally increases one's lifespan.

Well, it is not clear how positive thinking can scientifically affect our health. However, when we're able to cope better with stress and stay away from unhealthy behaviors, we can boost our overall well-being.

Positive Thinking Is Good For Your Health

It has been shown that having positive thinking helps increase our lifespan and gives us better feelings than those who have negative thought patterns. The truth is, all the negative thoughts that we have in our minds are mirrored on our bodies. In other words, when we are stressed and have depressive thoughts, we do not sleep better, and our muscles tend to tense up. We end up being anxious about the unknown, and we become dissatisfied with everything. However, when we work towards beating these negative emotions, we ward off the physical outcomes it has on our bodies, and we regain our health.

It Can Make You More Resilient

Resilience simply means one's ability to ensure difficult situations. In other words, when you face a traumatic situation with resilience, you have the strength and resolve to get through it. Instead of falling apart when faced with such situations, you pick up the pieces and move on to overcome the whole problem.

If you are an optimistic person, you will be able to look at the whole problem and find ways to address the issue wherever you can. In other words, rather than giving up hope, you marshal up your resources and free will to solve the problem. You go the extra mile to ask the people around you to help wherever they can.

According to research, there is evidence that shows that amid a crisis like a natural disaster or a terror, positive thoughts go a long way in providing a buffering system against issues such as depression, especially for people who have resilience. The good news is that positive thinking and resilience are traits that one can cultivate. When you nurture positive emotions, you are better positioned to reap both short-term and long-term rewards.

You Have Better Relationships With People

When you have positive thinking, you will have a better first impression on others. You must realize that people are more attracted to those who are positive mainly because they send the impression that they can maintain friendships. This may explain the reason why people with positive thinking have an active social life.

The same applies to romantic relationships. As such, people who have positive thinking and attitude tend to attract the attention of the opposite sex more than those are have a negative attitude and thinking.

More Focused And Concentrated

When you realize that the problem you are facing could have happened to anyone around you and has happened to others before, it is only then that you accept that it is not the end of the world. It is then that you learn to remain focused whenever you are faced with a difficult situation. And the secret is to always have positive thinking in all situations.

More Confidence

When you have positive thinking, you gain lots of confidence in yourself and your abilities. The truth is, with positive thinking, you appreciate the level of your abilities and do not try to become someone you are not. In other words, you learn to appreciate and love who you are, and this has a lot of impact on your self-confidence.

They Have A Happier Life

According to research, there is evidence that demonstrates that people who have positive thinking and live a life full of optimism often have a longer lifespan compared to those that do not. This is because they learn to see possibilities where others do not and hence, end up being more productive in life.

One thing that you must remember is the law of attraction. If you think positively, you will attract positive things in your life. Therefore, learn to be grateful for everything that you have in life. Rather than dwelling on problems, see possibilities in those problems and sooner than you think, your life will change for the better.

That said, you must bear in mind that having positive thinking is not about taking shortcuts in life. Yes, there are times when optimism has been shown to have a negative outcome. It is not about ignoring the reality just for the sake of the silver lining. Always try to make the most out of every bad situation but base it on your abilities.

It is true that bad things are bound to happen one way or another. At some point in life, you will be disappointed and hurt by the people around you. This does not mean that the world is up against you. Instead, you should accept that such things do happen and instead of working too hard to keep a grudge, look at the situation in a realistic manner. This way, your situation will be made better, and you will learn from every bad experience you encounter.

CHAPTER 3

HOW TO RECOGNIZE "BLUE" THOUGHTS

Chapter 3

How to Recognize "BLUE" Thoughts

The term "BLUE" serves as an acronym.

B- blaming

L- looking for the bad news

U- unhappy guessing

E- exaggeratedly negative

The truth is, these thoughts are extremely negative for them to be anything from the truth. One important thing that you must note is that we have over 70,000 thoughts every day. These thoughts often have a great impact on our emotions and the choices we make in life. While you cannot control any automatic thoughts that you have raced through your mind, you have the power to control how you respond to them.

When you believe in self-doubt, worry unnecessarily over things you cannot control, and ruminate on the negative events in your life, your mental strength is drained. The secret here is for you to turn every negative thought into something positive. The trick is to purposefully train the mind to have a different way of thinking that will help build your mental muscle.

When you decide to take control of your inner thoughts and thought process, you become much stronger than when you would ruminate on negative thoughts throughout the day. The stronger you get, the higher your chances of becoming kind, productive, and receptive. In other words, when you have a positive thought process, you create a positive cycle that changes your way of doing things and ultimately impacts your life with success and happiness.

So, how can you recognize these negative thoughts?

Blaming Myself

Yes, we all must take responsibility for our actions. However, while that is a good thing, excessively blaming yourself can be counterproductive. When you blame yourself too much, studies have shown that this hurts your mental health and is likely to bring about depression. Therefore, ensure that you stay alert for the times when you feel like everything that is going wrong is your fault and remember to take responsibility for your actions, without necessarily being too hard on yourself.

Looking For The Bad News

Have you ever had a perfect day with everything going your way and then something bad suddenly happens and ruins it all? Well, I bet we all have had those days. But the most important question is, what did you do after that? What did you focus your attention more on?

I do not know about you, but I kept on pondering on what had ruined the day. So many of us get caught up in one bad thing or break even when you have had over ten good breaks that day. However, you have to realize that when you dwell too much on the bad things, your mind will be captured in a rather dark place. When you realize that, at this point simply take a step back to have a realistic perspective of things. This way, you will create a balanced and realistic plan of action to be happy, even amid the bad breaks.

Unhappy Guessing

No one knows what is lying in wait for us in the future or better still tomorrow. You may be here predicting doom when so much good lies ahead of you in your future. Maybe you are going to give a presentation tomorrow at work, or you could be preparing for an exam. At the back of your mind, you are thinking of how you will embarrass yourself or how you are going to fail that exam and miss opportunities.

One thing that you must realize is that when you have unhappy guessing into your future, there is a high chance that you will start acting like it and eventually bring the prophecy to come to pass. Each time you have such unhappy guessing, replace them with quite the opposite. What if you give the most memorable and amazing presentation anyone has ever had? What if you sit that exam and ace it and get so much more opportunities beyond your wildest dreams?

There is always an opportunity that things will turn out much better than we imagine. Rather than choosing to focus on the negative, think of all the positive things that will come of your success. That will empower you to exert more effort, and hard work to whatever you are doing, and this will ultimately yield impeccable results and success.

Exaggeratedly Negative

When you tell yourself that the whole experience was a great disaster, it is somewhat a downward spiral. When you start to convince yourself that your job is a complete joke, you are headed in the wrong direction. The truth is negativity yield negative results. There is no way you are going to be successful if you are always going to think that you are bound to fail. It will not make any sense in sitting the exam if you already believe that you will fail. In other words, the more negative you feel, the worse you get, hence lowering your chances of having positive outcomes.

That said, you must purpose to turn those "BLUE" thoughts into positive thoughts. One better way to do this is to put yourself in a friend's shoe and imagine what you would advise them if they were going through what you are facing today. Therefore, when you find yourself having negative, self-defeating thoughts, think of a concrete and clear plan that will help redeem you to a better place in life.

You will realize that when you replace negative thoughts with more realistic positive thoughts it can be very inspiring and is the key for you to create the kind of life you want to live. If you choose to naturally err on the negative thinking end of the spectrum, it will take too much effort to change your thoughts. However, when you start changing them slowly, with time, your brain will physically change for the better. In other words, thinking positively will come naturally, and your brain will begin to perceive you and the abilities you have in a new light.

CHAPTER 4

WHAT NEGATIVE THOUGHTS DO TO YOUR BRAIN

Chapter 4

What Negative Thoughts Do To Your Brain

Over the years, the human brain has evolved and adapted to make decisions and thus respond quickly to safety threats. In this regard, when an individual stresses, worries, or adopts negative thinking, the human brain is tricked into believing that there is an immediate threat. Consequently, the fight and flight response is activated to address the current issue or threat.

The human brain is physiologically designed to address or respond to negative thoughts or threats promptly. In this regard, negative beliefs or negative feelings trigger the prompt response of the brain as it would if the individual faced imminent danger to their safety. When we think positively, the brain operates under the assumption that everything is running well and under control, and that no action is needed.

This is the opposite of the reaction to negative thoughts. However, most people dismiss negative thinking because it is typically not life-threatening. The core question here is: how many of the negative thoughts, worries, and stresses are life-threatening to the affected individual?

Recent studies focusing on the psychology of human beings reveal that negative thoughts that are resulting in stress are causing overuse of this powerful safety system, which is in turn leading to a weakening of the immunity system and thus causing a surge in the likelihood of people facing the disease.

This underscores the fact that negative thinking is causing more harm to our bodies as well as our brains than we realize.

According to the *Journal of Clinical Psychology*, negative thoughts and worrying have significant effects on the abilities of people to complete their day-to-day tasks. In this regard, people that worry 50 percent or more of the time display considerable disruption in their ability to address the difficult challenges they face daily as opposed to those with positive thinking.

Therefore, a surge in the levels of negative thoughts clouds the individual's ability to solve problems and the self-belief that is required to address some crucial tasks. When the brain is faced with intricate and complex tasks, negative thoughts have a disruptive impact on the individual's ability to process information and think with clarity.

In this regard, according to the researcher, accumulating negative thoughts regarding the challenges one is facing does not help them come up with any solutions, it makes it harder for such individuals to think of any problem-solving ideas or effective solutions. It shatters the confidence and self-belief that are the drivers of creativity and innovation, which form the basis of problem-solving mentalities.

The impact of negative thoughts includes effects on memory, the brain (amygdala and thalamus) as well as on the hormonal system, which control significant aspects involved in the discourse of understanding, conceptualizing, and addressing challenges. Therefore, the accumulation of negative thoughts affects your ability to see, self-esteem, self-confidence, and the bravery to address a challenge head-on with the hope that you will succeed.

Eliminating negative thoughts is crucial in improving the functioning of our brains. This can be achieved by focusing on positive thinking, which can be achieved through training of your brain to focus on the positive and opportunities that will appear at any moment.

The Link Between Thinking and Actions

According to *Psychology Today*, "Thoughts may come at whim, but actions are curbed by will." This statement establishes an important relationship between thoughts and actions while also pointing out the differences that separate the two concepts.

What one thinks typically comes from their experiences of their environment, what they learn, and how they interact with other people. Thoughts are often the raw feelings informed by each other's experiences and perceptions of the world. Additionally, they have limitless freedom regarding what they can think (whether negative or positive). However, actions are driven by will and typically are affected by their impact on other people within the local community, at work, or school.

Typically, the way you feel regarding yourself, your self-confidence, and self-esteem are the fundamental drivers of your thoughts. In many cases, these thoughts can transform into actions. The actions that you take are often the key ingredients of getting what you want in life. Therefore, if you are not achieving your goals as planned, it is essential to take some time and assess how you feel about yourself.

Meeting your targets in life involves repeated action(s) and persistence as well. Self-esteem is crucial in shaping the drive, determination, as well as personal power that are crucial in taking measures to achieve success. This highlights the power of positive thinking.

It forms the foundation of support, motivation, and self-confidence and esteem, which are crucial in driving the ability of an individual to meet their core targets in life, business, and at work. At the same time, negative thoughts are a massive dream killer. Telling yourself "I can't" will lower self-esteem and confidence, reduce the effectiveness of any of the core actions that you take, and thus prevent your ability to achieve your objectives.

Therefore, although there is a distinction between thoughts and actions, they have a vital link. On the one hand, one's movements are often impactful on the thought of an individual. In this case, negative actions will often lead to negative thoughts. On the other hand, the type of thinking you adopt (positive or negative) has a considerable impact on the ultimate actions an individual undertakes.

CHAPTER 5

TIPS TO TRAIN YOUR MIND FOR POSITIVE THOUGHTS

Chapter 5

Tips to Train Your Mind for Positive Thoughts

Subconscious Retraining

There are so many ways in which you can learn to release the negativity that has built up inside you and is holding you back. Some of these experiences are those that happened to you during your childhood that the body and the mind have held onto for years. These are the things that are inhibiting you from exploring your full potential.

Some of the exercises that will help retrain your subconscious include neuro-linguistic programming (NLP) and tapping among others. They play a central role in helping one access the subconscious part of the brain so that it can build more assertive and affirming beliefs.

Others have also used hypnotherapy and meditations to help them retrain their subconscious. In other words, when you do that, you are simply training the brain to let go of all the negative events in your past and rebuilding new positive events going forward into the future.

Set Aside Specific Time for What You Love

It is easy for us to say that we do not have time because of the many commitments both professionally and socially. However, we must create some time out of our busy schedules for the things we are passionate about. Otherwise, when we fail to make time and space for the things we love, we easily allow negativity and despondence to take a toll on us.

The trick is to ensure that you take the front seat in maintaining boundaries that will permit you to pursue your passion. Start by setting apart at least an hour every day without any interruptions by other obligations. Even if you have to say no to other things, be glad to do it for the sake of building a positive mindset.

Take Good Care Of Yourself

So many research studies have shown that the things we eat and drink greatly influences our emotional state just like our approach to sleep and exercise. Therefore, if you desire to have positive thinking, you must pay attention to what you feed your body with. This way, you can easily identify potential areas for improvement.

Ask yourself whether your diet is healthy and if it offers you the right minerals and nutrients for your body. Are there ways you can vary your diet for better health? From research, it is clear that vitamin deficiencies have an impact on our health and has been associated with anxiety and depression.

On the other hand, failing to get adequate sleep time at night has also been shown to have an impact on our thinking by naturally stimulating negative thoughts. When you start treating your physical body with care, both the mental and emotional centers will respond similarly.

Give Positivity To Feel The Positivity

Did you know that when you are kind to the people around you, they do not just become happy, but you also feel good about it? When you take a minute to do something nice to another person or even a stranger on the streets, you get in the right frame of mind. It is what will help you break free from negative thinking.

Therefore, make up your mind today to get in the habit of expressing compassion for the people that need it most each time you feel that you are anxious and hopeless. Soon enough, it will come naturally, and the times when you feel negative will last just a short time before it all fades away.

Focus On What Makes You Happy To Be Alive

The best way you can train your brain to embrace positive thinking is to ensure that you seek to repeatedly and deliberately focus on things that inspire happiness and joy. Start by getting a notebook dedicated for this and each morning you get up, record at least five things that inspire happiness and that you will focus on that day.

While you do this, you must think of various categories you can pay attention to. For instance, what are some of the interactions that bring you joy? Are there elements in the world around you that inspire you? Are there aspects in yourself that make you feel more confident and prouder? The truth is, when you pay attention to the things that make you happy, you are in effect, strengthening the neural pathways in your brain associated with positive thinking and having a positive attitude towards life.

Flip Negatives Into Positives

Finally, it is possible to retrain your brain in such a manner that it naturally chooses to see the bright side of things, irrespective of how tough the situation may be. At first, you will have to be deliberate about it so that you can challenge yourself to focus on the good in every bad encounter.

For instance, when something does not go as expected, it is better to think that the universe has something better in store for you. Learn from every experience instead of choosing to see yourself as a failure.

Additionally, you must try as much as you can to turn your setbacks into possibilities. If you did not land that job, instead of sulking and letting it weigh you down, think of ways you can do better next time. With time, you will realize that your brain will not wait around for promptings; it will simply do this automatically. In other words, your neural wiring will be on the lookout for more positive events and thoughts in your life.

CHAPTER 6

THE ROLE OF THE LANGUAGE WE USE

Chapter 6

The Role Of The Language We Use

The importance of language in positive thinking is underscored by the fact that thoughts are typically formulated in the form of language. This is especially the case during intimate conversations – issues or subjects that an individual thinks or even discusses with self.

Therefore, positive thinking is directly impacted by the type of language one adopts. For example, if one uses negative language, then it is difficult to maintain positive thoughts, which means that adopting a language that is encouraging and supportive helps establish a platform upon which positive thinking is built.

Positive Language

Speakers of the English language often have the option of choosing a positive statement or a negative statement in delivering the same meaning. For example, *"Come to the meeting on time"* and *"do not come to the meeting late"* both provide a similar message. However, the connotation behind the former statement is significantly less negative. This highlights the influence of language in the binary choice of either positive or negative sounding, which also applies to thoughts.

English is laden with several opportunities to formulate negative speech instead of more positive dialogue, and thus offers users a chance to choose the tone of their language and the depicted attitude and mentality as well. Consultants in the business sector argue that the choice of a positive language bolsters the ability of effective communication between 30 and 40 percent times than when a negative version of the language is utilized.

The choice of positive words (language) is crucial in shaping the type of thoughts and inner conversations that you have. Therefore, choosing positive words will help bolster positive thoughts in your mind. Encouraging supportive and triumphant ideas will inspire you towards positive conversations with your peers, family, and those you are working with as well.

Positive thinking also underpins a positive mentality and attitude, which is essential in encouraging progress in some of the issues you are facing at home, in the community, or at work. Therefore, this shows that the type of language or thoughts one adopts (positive or negative) have a significant impact on their behavior and mentality, which means that this choice affects their brain.

Positive And Negative Language And The Brain

Studies that focused on the functioning of the brain and its relationships with the words that an individual uses reveal that words have an impact on the brain and how it functions. For example, when you choose positive words such as "loving-kindness," "love," and "peace," you can modify your brain functions through the surge in cognitive reasoning and bolstering the activity in your frontal lobe.

In this case, maintain the use of positive words in an extended period can lead to the activation of motivational centers of the brain. This will lead to marked manifestations in your attitude, mentality, work ethic, and overall approach to specific tasks in life and work.

Alternatively, when you choose to use negative words consistently, you stand in the way of the production of certain neurochemicals which are crucial stress management. Therefore, negative words often lead to the surge in negative thoughts which in turn lead to the activation of the brain's fear center.

This induces the production of stress-producing hormones into the system. As a result, these neurotransmitters and hormones interrupt the flow of the reasoning and logic processes in the brain and thus disrupt the normal functioning of the brain.

Therefore, the choice of language has a significant impact on the overall thoughts that an individual adopts. Positive words bolster positive thoughts and vice versa. Additionally, positive thinking is crucial in establishing a hormonal balance in the brain that encourages motivation, a positive mindset, and the willingness to perform to the best of an individual's capacity.

On the other hand, negative thoughts are a significant drag on the functioning of the brain, which is manifested in the negative, demotivated, and stress-driven mentality that is dull and lacking in drive. To adopt positive thinking, there are several aspects that one must adopt. These are highlights by the significant characteristics of positive thinking, as discussed below.

Characteristics Of Positive Thinking

Monitoring Your Self-Talk

People typically talk to themselves consistently. In many cases, the external dialogue begins with the inner one. Therefore, positive thinking is characterized by the choice of positive language in the external conversation. This is because just like the internal dialogue influences the external exchange, our choice of language in the external dialogue will also affect the inner thoughts as well. Therefore, there is a need to choose a positive language in the way you dialogue externally, which will, in turn, shape the thinking you adopt into a positive one.

Establishing A Psychological Space

Positive thinking is essential in helping individuals to address unexpected events in their lives. For example, when something happens to a person out of the blue, it is typical to have a knee-jerk reaction that is often negative. This is especially the case when an individual has negative thinking. However, positive thinking establishes a psychological space that pauses, takes some deep breaths, and seeks more information before the knee-jerk reaction. Therefore, positive thinking allows you to be more measured and deliberate in handling different issues or meeting various events in life.

Moreover, this approach will enable you to create some distance between the subject event and your reaction. In many cases, in negative thinking, the line between the event and the reaction becomes blurred, which means that any logical thinking is inhibited because of the surge of subjectivity. Therefore, positive thinking allows for a considered reaction after weighing all the viable options from different perspectives.

Positive Responses

The view or perception of an event can be either positive or negative. However, by adopting positive thinking, you can see events in your life either through a positive perspective or at least a neutral one. Therefore, instead of placing blame on others, you can take ownership of your role in improving things.

Additionally, it helps you to communicate confidence and optimism to the rest consciously. Positive responses also help establish strong overarching relationships with others, which bolster happiness, positivity, and motivation of others. Such good relations also reflect on the self in the form of self-respect and self-confidence as well.

Become A Positive Contagion

Positive thinking plays a crucial role in shaping the mentality, attitude, and even behavior of an individual. People adopting positive thinking exude self-confidence and the trust of others to do the right thing. This is especially important because we tend to mirror the people whom we spend the most time with. This underscores the need to make sure that when people mirror you, they display positive thinking, healthy behavior, and a motivated mentality as well. The underlying aim here is to lift others as opposed to bringing them down.

The Importance of Positive Language

Positive language highlights what you can do as opposed to what you cannot do. It also highlights a caring mentality, focuses on the individual abilities as opposed to the disabilities, and overall seeks to highlight success as opposed to failure.

In spoken language, it helps inspire, encourage, support, and motivate others to achieve the best they can. In thoughts, positive language is crucial in highlighting individual competencies and thus helps to establish self-esteem, confidence, and belief that are crucial in achieving laid out targets and overcoming challenges as well.

Positive thinking comes in the form of "what succeeds" as opposed to "what fails." Therefore, this mentality is "problem-solving" because it highlights areas where you can help, repair, improve, enhance, or fix the current challenges. It magnifies the individual's capacity to solve the difficulties, which helps inspire the coming up of solutions, minimizing the discouraging fear, and bolstering motivation even in the face of adversity.

The Relationship Between Positive Thinking and a Positive Attitude

A positive attitude is desired in many aspects of life at home, in the community, and at work. Therefore, there is a need to actively pursue the nurturing and development of such attitude to bolster your chances of success at work, relationships, and relating to social constructs in the community.

In many ways, positive thinking plays a central role in the adoption and development of a positive attitude. However, it is essential to note that positive thinking is not a naturally occurring concept of life; instead, it is a conscious choice that an individual adapts to influence their life in a targeted way. Therefore, a positive attitude can be acquired through the adoption of a positive thinking approach and the overarching perception of the world as well.

Some of the ways one can adopt a sustainable and effective positive attitude include reading motivating and inspiring stories regarding people that have achieved success. This will motivate and inspire you as well as show you the areas in which they succeeded in making the right choices that led them to success.

Using affirmations, creating mental scenes of success, and actively avoiding negative thoughts to thrive in your mind will establish a platform for positive thinking and thus a positive attitude. Moreover, adopting a pro-active lifestyle will help you to avoid getting negative. If you keep yourself busy, the chances of developing and harboring negative thoughts will be markedly reduced.

Therefore, this section highlights the importance of positive thinking to be its influence on the attitudes and behaviors of the subject individual. In this regard, positive thinking bolsters the development of positive behaviors characterized by motivation, self-confidence as well as supportive behavior.

CHAPTER 7

STEPS ON HOW TO TRAIN YOUR MIND TO THINK POSITIVE

Chapter 7

Steps On How To Train Your Mind To Think Positive

Step 1: Observe Your Thoughts

The first step to training your mind to think positively is observing your thoughts. The truth is, most of the negative thoughts we have often creep in at a certain time, place, or during special events in your life. This may be explained by the fact that we are creatures of habit. For instance, you may be anxious whenever you have a trip coming up. Or you may be stressed because you have an interview up ahead of you. Or it may be that what is causing you to be upset is because you had a major fight with your spouse.

The moment you know the negative thoughts that keep bothering you, it will be easy to devise a plan to resolve the problem. For instance, if it is a job interview that is causing you stress, you will simply start preparing early and asking people who have attended similar interviews for advice.

Everything starts from your thoughts, so be on the lookout for negative thoughts and their possible triggers.

Step 2: Scan For The Three Daily Positives

Every single day, we have experiences and encounters, some of which are negative while others are positive. Therefore, before you decide to go to bed, you can make it a habit to reflect on three positive encounters you had that day. It can range from someone buying you coffee at work, watching the sunset with your husband, or landing a new client. It can also be small things like a compliment from a coworker/friend, bumping into an old friend, making a new friend, or watching your kids play. All these are more than enough to make you happy.

Step 3: Give Someone A Shout-Out

Gratitude is important. According to research, gratitude can make one optimistic and can even help ward off heart disease. The best place to start is by keeping a gratitude journal where you record all the things you are grateful for every single day. However, I have discovered that sharing gratitude is far much fulfilling and satisfying in life than just writing it down.

Here, you can record anything from just thanking yourself, child or spouse for all the hard works, complimenting your friend, having a discussion with your spouse about how their day was. This may feel a little weird at first, but with time, you will appreciate just how awesome it feels to give someone a shout-out.

Step 4: Help Others

Each day is an opportunity for us to help someone in need. Most people think that helping someone is only about giving them money. However, helping others may take any form from just helping a friend organize their work/project to helping a colleague with invoicing. It may be helping someone in the kitchen with the cooking or the dishes. It may be holding the door for someone, buying a stranger a cup of coffee as well as volunteering among others. Just find anything that you can do for someone today. Daily, try putting a smile on someone's face and watch what positivity that has in your life.

Step 5: Surround Yourself With Positive People

Did you know that emotions are contagious? Imagine walking into a room happy and jovial, and you find people gloomy and sad. What effect will that have on you after having a meeting with them for an hour or so?

The truth is, you will leave that room feeling worse than you found them. So, it is important that you pay attention to the people that you interact and spend most of your time with. If you spend time with people who like complaining and blaming others, you will soon be doing the same. Therefore, the only thing that makes sense is you surrounding yourself with people who inspire you to be a better person, giver, lover, and friend.

Step 6: Look After Your Body And Mind

Based on research findings, it is evident that when you take good care of yourself both physically and mentally, this will influence happiness and satisfaction in your life. It is through this that your mind will learn to think positively with time.

For instance, when you eat healthily and work out regularly, the body will tend to release feel-good hormones that will lift your mood and change your general outlook of life. One of the best ways you can train the mind to practice positive thinking is by meditating and practicing mindfulness through yoga.

Mindfulness is one of the most important steps in helping you stay aware of your thoughts and feelings without necessarily passing judgment on whether they are good or bad. One of the ways you can practice mindfulness is setting three separate alarms throughout the day. When the buzzer goes on, you simply stop what you are doing to take a deep breath. This goes a long way in restoring balance and positivity to your life.

Step 7: Let Go Of All The Negativity So That You Can Have Inner Healing

One of the tricks of becoming positive is uncovering all the negative thoughts we have and then releasing them all. Do not try to hold back; just let them go one after the other. It is these negative thoughts that often bring us pain and wounds in our lives, and we can never progress if we cannot let go of these degrading thoughts. It is only when we are able to free ourselves from negative thoughts, we are able to build a new system of affirming beliefs that can empower our future.

Step 8: Make Time To Do Something That You Love

This is easier said than done. However, it is one of the most important steps of winning back positivity into your life. Start by looking around you to determine the things that you enjoy doing. The truth is, the action does not matter, but what counts is that you love it. This could be reading, singing, teaching, sports, movies, or cooking, among others.

Start by setting aside time each day from just an hour to focus on the things you love. Free up some time to do something that you genuinely love and enjoy. These are some of the things that impact your happiness and fulfillment in life, and you do not want to miss out on them. Try to fix it at the time when you have the least amount of distractions. Within no time, you will realize how that changes your thinking to one with more positivity than you ever thought possible.

CHAPTER

8

THINKING SYSTEMS FOR SUCCESS – PLANNING POSITIVE FUTURE

Chapter 8

Thinking Systems For Success – Planning Positive Future

Progress in human life is typically constituted of overcoming challenges and hurdles in life. Therefore, for one to succeed, they must solve the challenges and problems they face personally in their lives as well as in the external environment. There is a need to engage with the environment, which is highly influenced by the ability of the subject individual to think and assess the current climate, their capacity, and subsequently come up with solutions.

However, the challenge to this approach is the natural predisposition of human beings to using shortcuts. Every time there is an alternative (quick, cheap, and easy) way to achieve something, people typically adopt it. This negatively affects their ability to think outside the box and come up with solutions as well.

The underlying basis of success in the short, medium, and long-term is developing good habits deliberately aimed at achieving success. However, good practices constitute more than just having a checklist lifted from a book. Instead, it is about nurturing and developing winning systems that become natural to you (second nature) and work towards the targeted goals of success.

However, coming up with the right systems, thinking to overcome challenges and achieve success is not straight forward because of the unpredictability, volatility, ambiguity, and complexity of the world. Overcoming the uncertainty of life cannot be achieved by gaining more control. Instead, developing agility, increased speed of learning, accelerated thinking, innovation, and creativity, will allow one to adapt and adjust every time the inevitable evolutions and changes occur.

Some of the significant areas of systems thinking and planning for success are discussed below.

Addressing Failure

In the pursuit of success, failure is often experienced. Most of the people that have succeeded in life have experienced different types of failure at various points of their life and the process of success. Therefore, there is considerable value in paying attention to the people that have succeeded and turned their lives into a success story.

In many cases, successful people are just like us. They have experienced many failures. The difference is that they kept working on their ideas, refining the process until they finally succeeded.

Success is typically achieved through the application of precise and detailed systems that are subsequently followed strictly and the same way every time. However, this approach to systems thinking faces the challenge of a continually evolving and changing external environment. This means that the approach adopted by one individual to achieve success might not be as effective for another individual because they will be facing different external environment dynamics.

However, it is essential to realize that the way we choose to address and complete a task is often the most difficult. As a result, this highlights the need to pause and reflect on the tasks at hand, objectives, and then choose the most effective way to achieve targets efficiently. People don't immediately identify the most efficient methods and ways to accomplish the same work. This underscores the need for reflection and deep thought in designing the best way forward to optimize not only performance but also reward.

Moreover, it is paramount to always be on the lookout for ways to improve performance, including through creativity and innovation. Experimentation and tinkering are a crucial part of this process because it allows you to determine the methods to finish the job and accomplish great work as well.

Developing A Winning Formula

The winning formula refers to the approach adopted by an individual to gain success in the targeted areas of life or business. In many cases, a winning method begins with positive thinking. There is a need to adopt a positive attitude towards both the methods adopted as well as the objectives of the project.

This way, you place yourself in a mentality that seeks to solve problems, innovate, and create ways to success as opposed to negative thinking that picks out the potential problems and therefore tones down the enthusiasm required to succeed. A positive thinking approach and attitude also rub off on the surrounding people. This helps create a motivated, targeted, and precise approach and environment that bolsters the chances of success.

Additionally, a winning formula is typically precise and targeted. This narrows down the areas of focus, which is essential in enhancing creativity and innovation to increase the chances of success. Doing things in the right way is also a fundamental aspect in achieving success. In many ways, "the right way" includes treating others positively, encouraging and motivating others, and seeing the best in the opportunities and even challenges. Therefore, positive thinking helps establish an overall environment that supports and drives success at an individual and collective level.

Establishing Your Systems

Developing a personalized system for thinking, planning, and innovating is crucial in bringing you closer to your goals. This requires a deep insight into and understanding of self as well as identifying how to shape and coach yourself regarding your approach to life. This includes getting rid of your daily inner conversations of negative thoughts and worries and replacing them with positive thinking.

The target here is making things as easy as possible for yourself while also ensuring that you accomplish your responsibilities and goals. Therefore, it is vital to give yourself the luxury of thinking about how you can do things in a better way. Some of the means of developing and sustaining a winning system are discussed below.

Understanding And Assessing Your Process

It is essential to understand your thinking system before you can go about fixing it. This allows you to establish an overall and deep understanding of your strengths and weaknesses, as well as how you operate. Spending time to get to know yourself is a crucial step in establishing your position in the thinking system.

Evaluating your process is important as well. For example, if you are staying up until 1 a.m. it could mean that you do not have enough sleep and thus having trouble getting up. Therefore, self-assessment will allow you to understand the aspects that are working and contributing towards your success as well as those that are holding you back. The resulting priority will enhance your capacity to succeed.

Studying Others And Their Actions

Researching what other people are doing is essential in shaping and developing both your thinking system as well as progress towards success. Therefore, whether it is a mentor, someone you admire, or an individual that is famously successful, it is important to find how they do things. Learn some crucial lessons of their thinking systems, approaches, attitudes, behavior, and mentalities as well.

There is nothing wrong with using what is already available to achieve success. If you can utilize someone else's thinking system or positive thinking to achieve success, then go for it. Moreover, you can tweak what you need to fit your specific needs as well as the prevailing external environment to optimize the chances of achieving success.

Anticipating Challenges

Hurdles and challenges typically characterize the road to success. Therefore, the ability to surmount some of these difficulties is the marker of success. Challenges that are anticipated are often half-solved. This means that if you see a problem coming, it is easier to prepare and come up with a solution compared to when a problem surprises you.

This underscores the importance of anticipating challenges. Developing the foresight of understanding the medium to long-term future is important. It is also essential to establish the implications of such dynamism. It places you at a very advantageous position to surmount such difficulties.

Aside from the preparatory advantages, such anticipation allows you to change and adapt in a manner that not only avoids the negative effects of change. It also harnesses such change forces and turns them into a value-creating opportunity.

Adaptability and flexibility are remarkable because change is constant. Without agility, the capacity to sustain success is diminished. This is because the external environment is continually changing, and thus demanding that individuals adapt their approach to achieving success. It is also essential to maintain honesty and openness with yourself to recognize and admit where your process breaks down. Making attempts, even when you experience failure, is crucial to build systems for success and ultimately succeed.

Conclusion

'*Change your thoughts, and you change your world,*' Norman Vincent Peale. There you have it. The most effective ways to change your life is ensuring that you employ a positive mindset. It may sound straightforward and yet you must read this whole book to find it easier to have positive thinking.

Now you know what positive thinking is and the power of thinking positively. At this point, you know how to move from a negative mindset to have a positive thinking and a positive attitude. One thing that you must understand is that positive thinking only forms the first half of the power of your mind.

The other half of the power lies in the actions that you take once you have positive thoughts. This is the point where your willpower comes in to play. It is your willpower that determines whether things will get done or not. It is this willpower that corresponds to the inner voice that tells us to act for our thoughts to come into reality.

Realize that your mind and willpower are not distinct from each other. If you don't see it in your mind, you can never manifest it in reality. You must have a completely positive mindset and conviction that you belong there and that you will achieve any dream you desire.

To do that, you will have to shut down all the negative thoughts and self-talk that tell you otherwise. The best you can do is to overpower this negativity with a triple dose of positivity. You simply tell yourself that you are strong enough and have the confidence it takes to win. This way, you will focus on the nitty-gritty of your performance in the ring. By tapping into the wells of positive thinking, attitude, abilities, and skills, you become unstoppable in and outside the ring. That is what life is all about; positivity for happiness and satisfaction!

Printed in Great Britain
by Amazon

57128119R00046